RENTAL PROPERTY SUCCESS

JOSH KATTENBERG WITH **DEREK KATTENBERG**

Copyright © 2014 by Josh Kattenberg

ISBN: 978-0-9895244-3-8

All rights reserved. No part of this book may be reproduced or transmitted in any form or by any means, electronic or mechanical, including photocopying, recording or by any information storage and retrieval system, without permission in writing from the copyright owner. For information on distribution rights, royalties, derivative works or licensing opportunities on behalf of this content or work, please contact the publisher at the address below.

Printed in the United States of America.
Design by Paperback, paperbackdesign.com

Although the author and publisher have made every effort to ensure that the information and advice in this book was correct and accurate at press time, the author and publisher do not assume and hereby disclaim any liability to any party for any loss, damage, or disruption caused from acting upon the information in this book or by errors or omissions, whether such errors or omissions result from negligence, accident, or any other cause.

Josh Kattenberg – Owner, Real Property Management Express
605.274.7373   josh@expressrpm.com

RENTAL PROPERTY SUCCESS

Horror Stories, Insider Secrets
and Disciplines of Successful
Rental Property Owners

JOSH KATTENBERG WITH **DEREK KATTENBERG**

THRONE
PUBLISHING GROUP

TABLE OF CONTENTS

INTRODUCTION	7
1. PROFITABLE INVESTORS	**8**
HABITS OF PROFITABLE INVESTORS	16
2. QUESTIONS TO ASK BEFORE YOU INVEST	**18**
3. COMMON COSTLY MISTAKES	**26**
HOW CAN A GOOD INVESTMENT GO BAD?	54
4. THE COST OF OVERLOOKED DETAILS	**56**
LEGAL AND PROCESS CHECKLIST	66
5. MAINTENANCE SECRETS THAT $AVE	**68**
6. INSIDER SECRETS FOR MAXIMIZING YOUR INVESTMENT	**76**
7. QUESTIONS FOR QUALIFYING A PROPERTY MANAGER	**88**
8. RENT YOUR HOME QUICKLY	**96**
9. CONSISTENTLY RECEIVING RENT PAYMENTS	**100**
DO'S AND DON'TS FOR QUALIFYING GOOD TENANTS	106
7 TIPS TO AVOID TENANT TROUBLE	108
NEXT STEPS	110
SUGGESTED READING	112
ABOUT THE AUTHORS	114

INTRODUCTION

Simply put, there are things we know and things we do not know.

What you don't know can cause significant harm to you and your family, especially when it comes to investing in rental properties. Passion and excitement mixed with inexperience and lack of council can lead to major problems, including permanent damage to your family's financial future.

As a successful owner of a Real Property Management franchise, my colleges and I currently manage 10s of thousands of properties and several billion in real estate assets. Over the past 25 years we have witnessed the following far too often. A successful family considers investing in a rental property as part of their future retirement plan. They find the right house at just the right time and make an offer, never taking a moment to account for the many evening and weekend hours their new investment will require. Inevitably, the property becomes a second job that demands more time and nets less money than a full-time job. This may seem like an exaggeration, but it happens far too often to individuals and families who do not know enough about the rental property business. With the right team and wise council, however, it is absolutely possible to create a secure future and solid investment portfolio with rental properties.

This book is my attempt to give you access to the years of experience my team and I have gained from managing thousands of properties. We've helped many become successful, and we've watched many fail. By reading this book, it is my hope that you will protect and empower yourself to make the right decision at the right time while building a powerful future legacy for your family.

Josh Kattenberg
CEO/Owner, Real Property Management Express
605.274.7373
josh@expressrpm.com

CHAPTER
Profitable Investors

If there was ever an industry that experienced Murphy's Law, it is the real estate business. Truly, anything that can go wrong will go wrong. What do you need to be prepared for? Anything and everything. You will make mistakes, there will be trouble, and you will more than likely lose money at some point. Profitable investors realize this, and they distinguish themselves from their unprofitable counterparts through their education, discipline, and realistic expectations. They regard their rental property or properties in the same manner as a small business owner thinks of their business entity. A business owner accounts for all costs, researches his or her industry, and systematically executes a plan based on proven results. If you think the same way about your real estate investments, you are on the right track toward profitable real estate investing.

There are three basic building blocks from which you can build a solid foundation for real estate success.

EDUCATION

Profitable investors have actively sought and received formal education directly relating to the real estate industry. If you ask them, they will be able to tell you about the seminar they attended, the books they've read, and the podcast interviews to which they've listened. They treat their real estate investment like a profession because to them, it is a profession, and professionals are the only people who make money.

> **They treat their real estate investment like a profession, because professionals are the only people who make money.**

These educated investors understand that iron sharpens iron. They continually communicate with other successful investors within their market, frequent local real estate investment meetings, and know the key players in the industry. Through these events, they not only acquire peer-to-peer coaching, but also build relationships with potential mentors and investing partners. I strongly encourage you to find a mentor. Mentorship in real estate, or any other profession for that matter, is vital to success and often makes the difference between the winners and losers. I am constantly learning and seeking out better ways to do things. I study people's habits and practices and try to implement them into my habits and life.

For your real estate investment, your education will take time as well as commitment to personal growth. Profitable investors understand their portfolio grows in direct proportion to their personal growth, so patience balanced with urgency is essential in achieving investment success. Keep in mind that it typically takes five years working full-time in the business before you become an expert, or as Malcolm Gladwell has taught us, it takes approximately 10,000 hours to master your craft.

DISCIPLINE

I've always believed that discipline is simply doing what must be done, whether you feel like it or not. It is the ability to give yourself a command and get the job done. A disciplined person follows through on his or her word at all times.

In real estate, discipline translates into fully understanding your investment goals and surrounding yourself with the right tools and skills to successfully achieve those goals. Before a profitable investor creates a plan or buys any property, he or she diligently answers the following questions, and so should you:

Will your investment model focus on single family or multi-family property?

What type of tenants do you plan to target?

Will you invest using personal capital, a loan, or by working together with partners?

Will you invest in aged properties which require more maintenance, or will you purchase new properties?

What is your investment strategy and model?

Once you have answered these questions, you are ready to create a solid business plan. While business plans typically involve more work than originally anticipated, they do provide the necessary time and due diligence to count the cost of your prospective endeavor before you waste even more time and potentially lots of money.

> **Managing real estate is an emotional business, and profitable investors rely on data to keep them grounded, directed, and in control of their emotions.**

With an investment strategy and business plan in place, you are now in a position to begin making decisions based on data rather than on emotions. Managing real estate is an emotional business, and profitable investors rely on data to keep them grounded, directed, and in control of their emotions. This, of course, is easier said than done. People are emotional about their money and collecting rent is a stressful business, but there is no margin for grace in property management. For example, if someone doesn't pay rent on time, they must be dealt with using no uncertain terms, just like someone who attempts to shoplift a bag of chips needs to be kicked out of the store immediately. The same goes with making difficult decisions. It is much easier to extend timelines, but in this business, time truly is money and can make or break you. There is no room for passivity.

By disciplining their emotions, their mind, and their plans, profitable investors create realistic expectations and a system for winning.

EXPECTATIONS

Profitable investors don't let their excitement blur the numbers. While you will have high emotions in this business, your emotions should not lead your decision making. Instead, make your choices based on data, and then use your emotions to drive your actions. While the earning capacity for investment properties is great, wise and profitable investors don't expect to put $1,000 down and get rich in a year. They realize that in order to experience a profit in the business, they must assume risk and maintain a long-term vision.

> *Profitable investors don't let their excitement blur the numbers.*

Much of what is done in real estate is basic risk management. Your job is to manage those risks, limit them, and put the odds in your favor as much as possible. There should be a disclaimer for investing in real estate just like the stock market. The desire to win must be tempered with caution and wisdom. You won't win 100% of the time in real estate, just like in business or stocks, so you must be realistic in your expectations and resolute with your actions.

John C. Maxwell said, "Humility is what allows us to recognize and learn from our mistakes. It is the quality that makes the difference between the person who fails and falls, and the person who stumbles, gets up and never repeats the same mistake."

Education, discipline, and realistic expectations are fundamental to finding success in the real estate industry. Utilizing these three points, you will build a solid investment foundation, distinguish yourself as a profitable investor, and create a legacy you and your family will enjoy for years to come.

> *"Humility is what allows us to recognize and learn from our mistakes. It is the quality that makes the difference between the person who fails and falls, and the person who stumbles, gets up and never repeats the same mistake."*

Habits of Profitable Investors

HABIT 1

TAKE TOTAL RESPONIBILITY. Profitable investors take total responsibility for their investments. Unprofitable investors blame everything and everyone else: The property manager, Wall Street, the government, etc. Build a relentless attitude and nothing can stop you. It's your money, your risk, your work… And Your Success!

HABIT 2

KNOW YOUR NUMBERS. If your accounting is off or not up-to-date, you will make decisions based on emotions and not on numbers which will eventually hurt you in the long run. Data and numbers help you learn, adapt and plan for long term success.

HABIT 3

READ SOMETHING NEW EVERY DAY. Successful people read constantly, find mentors to learn from, and value new information that can help propel them forward. Regardless the industry, you must learn before you earn. Learn your product, customers and competition. And then keep learning.

HABIT 4

REGULAR ASSESSMENTS. Regular assessments are essential to maintaining and protecting your investment. Visit your rental unit once per quarter, but you must do this in a way that doesn't unsettle your tenant while also creating some accountability. Do not limit assessments to the property. You must assess your accountant, tax advisor, property manager, forms, systems, and more. Professionals spend time assessing their entire investment system, not just the buildings in the portfolio.

HABIT 5

NEVER GIVE UP. Habitual personal growth is what separates the rock stars from the backup singers. On a personal note, I have noticed that *I am* the number one hurdle that separates me from the growth of my company. Do I have the vision for my company to be a multi-million dollar entity? Absolutely, but I may not yet have the skillset to manage that kind of capital. My ability to grow, learn and adapt will be the difference between million-dollar growth or staying where I am today. None of us lack the opportunity for greatness, we only lack the personal preparation necessary to seize the day and make it happen.

CHAPTER 2
Questions to Ask Before You Invest

WHAT OUTCOME DO YOU WANT TO ACHIEVE WITH YOUR REAL ESTATE INVESTMENT(S)?

Start working today with your ultimate goal in mind. Your long-term goals will influence your short term decision making. For example, are you investing in your property(s) with a long term or short term strategy? Are you going to hold them for 5 years or 30 years? The answers to these questions have massive implications in terms of how you manage your property.

For example, if your goal is to hold a property for 30 years and then cash out for retirement, you might consider locking in a 30-year mortgage. In addition, you will have a more strategic long-term approach to maintenance of the property. You can compare this to investing in an IRA account which cannot be touched until after retirement. Your end goal will cause you to think longer term and execute different strategies as opposed to a short term strategy such as "flipping" a house, whereby you fix up the property and sell it for a quick profit.

Let's frame this up by thinking about re-shingling the roof. If you are thinking in terms of a 30-year investment, you would use a more expensive, high-quality shingle that will last 30+ years, rather than buying a cheap, low-grade shingle that will have a shorter lifespan. If you plan to sell in 5 years, you are not worried about the shape the shingles will be in 30 years from today.

Your vision and the outcome you hope to achieve influences everything else you do, from maintenance, to capital improvements, to your mortgage. Set your goals, build a crystal clear mental vision of your success, and then create your plan for today with the future in your mind's eye.

WHAT EXPERIENCE DO YOU HAVE IN THE INDUSTRY?

Owning a rental property involves many disciplines. The more experienced you are in these disciplines, the more profitable you will be and the faster it will happen.

Investing in real estate is like football. To succeed you need a strong and driven team. Hiring the right professionals to be on your team will make the difference between success and failure. It's the same process someone goes through when starting a business. A smart entrepreneur seeks to build a team which includes an accountant, attorney, banker, IT person, and an insurance agent as the foundational members of their team. These are the minimum team members any business owner must have.

Establish a discovery process that will help you determine who will be a necessary and good fit for your team. Interview each professional and find individuals who understand the industry and your goals, have the ability to help you meet those goals, and can help you avoid the common pitfalls of owning rentals.

> *Interview each professional and find individuals who can help you avoid the common pitfalls of owning rentals.*

If you decide to include a rental property management company on your team, ask questions about their policies and be aware of their accounting practices and how it could adversely affect you and your investment goals.

REAL STORIES: GOOD RECORD KEEPING
For example, a property owner named Jeff used a rental management company whose accounting practices left him in a lurch. Jeff was in the process of trying to sell his rental property, and the potential buyer wanted to know if the property was profitable. In reviewing the accounting statement for the previous year, the prospective buyer noted an $11,000 miscellaneous maintenance expense listed and was concerned whether that was a one-time or recurring expense. Unfortunately, when Jeff asked his property manager to itemize this miscellaneous expense, the property management company's records were so vague that no one had any idea what the expense was for or why it had been assessed causing the buyer to walk away from the deal.

HOW MUCH TIME DO YOU EXPECT TO SPEND ON THIS INVESTMENT OVER THE FIRST 12 MONTHS? OVER THE NEXT 5 YEARS?

Owning a rental property can be time consuming, and without a property manager, it WILL be absolutely time consuming. Many experienced investors suggest doubling the time you project spending on your future investment, and if you are still willing to put in that amount of time, the investment makes sense. The rental business isn't a "get rich quick" scheme. It takes work, training, teamwork, and more to make it a profitable investment in your portfolio.

> *The rental business isn't a "get rich quick" scheme.*

Of course, there are ways to reduce the projected time spent managing both the property and its tenants, but it requires you to build systems and automations to streamline the processes. For example, some landlords drive around and pick up rent. While this method certainly works and pressures tenants to pay right away, this method is extremely time consuming and costly. Instead, train tenants on the rent due date, the consequences of paying late, and the legal ramifications of non-payment of rent. Another possibility is that you can have a system set up where an automatic payment is taken out on the first of the month.

With the aid of an attorney, the ramifications of late rent can be written out clearly in the lease and have legal consequences.

DOES YOUR REAL ESTATE AGENT HAVE EXPERIENCE IN RENTAL PROPERTIES?

Your real estate agent must have experience in rental properties, not just selling homes. As with any major decision or investment, it is best to seek council from an experienced expert who can give you an objective opinion before you spend any money. If your real estate agent understands rental properties, they will be one more resource from whom you can draw knowledge and mentorship.

However, I would not recommend using a real estate agent to source your first tenant. While they are technically licensed to provide this service, they will likely be less focused on renting your unit for a $400 commission when they may have properties for sale with a $10,000 commission at stake. You must be proactive in finding that first tenant as vacancies cost you money.

HOW MUCH CASH WILL YOU HAVE ON HAND FOR UNEXPECTED VACANCIES IN THE FIRST YEAR?

You should never depend solely upon the rent to pay the mortgage. You need to have a reserve, so that if the tenant leaves or does not pay rent for any reason, you can still cover at the very least two months of the mortgage. Each day the property sits vacant costs you money in lost rent and utilities. Protect your investment, and make sure you have alternative options.

HOW FAMILIAR ARE YOU WITH YOUR AREA'S HOUSING LAWS AND REGULATIONS?

You must read the laws and regulations of your state pertaining to rental property. Familiarize yourself with Federal and State Fair Housing Law as well as HUD (US Department of Housing and Urban Development) regulations on certain areas of concern such as lead based paint and other environmental hazards. This is certainly not glamorous or exciting work, but it's better than dealing with government officials when they bust you for a HUD violation, causing you to lose both profit and potential tenants.

CHAPTER 3
Common Costly Mistakes

FAILURE TO UNDERSTAND THE COST OF VACANCY

Rental property owners certainly understand that vacancies stop revenue, but many do not understand exactly how much money it costs them each day the property is vacant. Failing to understand your personal cost of vacancy will not only create long term financial issues for your business, but also potential problems for your family and wallet. You must know your numbers and make all decisions based on numbers. Do not base your finances on your emotional responses.

Here's how it works: Vacancy cost is a function of time. The more time a property sits vacant, the more money it will cost you.

Below is an example of a single family home renting for $1,000 per month.
- *Monthly rent = $1,000*
- *Daily rent = $33.33*
- *Annual rent = $12,000*
- *The maximum annual rent is $12,000.*
- *If the property is vacant for one month out of the year, annual rent*

falls to $11,000 or $917/mo.
- If vacant for two months, annual rent would be $10,000 or $833/mo.
- Each day the property sits vacant is costing the property owner: $33.33

This does not account for other costs you must continue to maintain while the property sits vacant. For example, the utilities must be turned on and running. Many property owners think that while no one is living at the property, the cost of utilities will be negligible. Quite the contrary. If the property is vacant in the winter, the heat must be kept at a reasonable temperature to keep pipes from freezing. Furthermore, the temperature must be set within a normal range during all seasons because the home needs to feel inviting to prospective tenants. The comfort of the home is part of the curb appeal. For example, realtors will "stage" vacant homes with fake furniture and wall hangings to give it a homey feel. Some home sellers even go so far as to bake cookies right before a showing to add the aroma of "home" to the experience. While I am not suggesting staging a home or baking cookies for a rental property, I am saying that the A/C and heat must be kept within comfortable levels, and utilities must be added to the cost of vacancy.

> *In the goal achieving process that accompanies successful rental property investment, you must have a sense of urgency.*

You also have additional risks during vacancy such as vandalism, storm damage, or a water leak that goes unreported. Rental property owners who fail to account for such possible major expenses are simply setting themselves up for setback and failure.

In the goal achieving process that accompanies successful rental property investment, you must have a sense of urgency. Without a sense of urgency, tomorrow becomes next week which becomes next month and so on. Your work will always expand to fit the time allocated for it. Understanding the daily cost of vacancy of your property will give you a higher level of urgency when you experience vacancy.

FAILURE TO SET A REASONABLE RENTAL PRICE

All property owners must fight the urge to overprice their rentals as they initially list the property on the market. It is a natural impulse to seek the most amount of money possible, but when we break down the numbers, we see that listing a property and finding a tenant quickly is the best possible scenario.

You see, rent prices are controlled by supply and demand. If your rental property is priced above the current market value, more competitively priced properties will rent while your overpriced property sits vacant, costing you money. Several things happen to the overpriced property:

1. Even if you eventually get the asking price, because your property has been vacant for 1-2 months, you did not actually receive your asking price (remember the cost of vacancy). If you were asking $1,000 per month but the property was vacant for two months, you will actually only receive an average of $833 per month over a 12 month period.

2. Overpriced properties turn off qualified tenants. Once a prospective tenant calls about the property and finds it is overpriced, he or she will cross the property off the list, look elsewhere, and not come back. Even if the rental price is lowered a few weeks later, those tenants will have already rented a property or will not know that the price has been lowered.

3. The rental agent or property manager will eventually get frustrated showing a property that is overpriced and therefore un-leasable. They will quickly tire of spending time and money showing a property that tenants simply will not rent due to the current price. In addition, as every salesperson knows, to be a good sales person, you must believe in your product. It is hard to believe in a product that you know is overpriced.

If you have a system for getting your home rented quickly, if and when it becomes vacant, you will not have to deal with the above issues. The key is to have a proven system so you are not stuck guessing or emotionally reacting. Proven systems are the absolute difference between profits and losses when it comes to rental properties.

When selling real estate, home owners can often afford to wait until they receive their asking price. Their property may appreciate, they may continue to make monthly principle payments, or they continue to live in the property while it is listed. Conversely, a rental property owner will never recover the revenue lost during the vacancy of a rental. With that said, you must have a proven system that allows you to rent your property as fast as possible, to the right people, at the right time.

FAILURE TO PERFORM CONSISTENT ASSESSMENTS

Quarterly walk-through assessments can help eliminate not only the worry of owning rentals, but also the actual damage caused by a neglectful tenant. A walk-through assessment is not the same thing as the type of inspection done by a trained and licensed home inspector that is completed before the purchase of your rental property. Instead, a walk-through assessment quickly allows the owner to examine the inside and outside of the property to determine if the tenant is abiding by the terms of the lease and to catch any minor maintenance concerns before they become big problems. You or your property manager can easily conduct this type of walk-through.

A walk-through assessment quickly allows the owner to examine the inside and outside of the property to determine if the tenant is abiding by the terms of the lease.

Remember to give your tenant at least a 24-hour notice of the walk-through, and mention the items you will be checking (furnace filters, air conditioning, etc.) so the tenant is not surprised or alarmed. Without giving proper notice, you could be trespassing. Be courteous and respectful; after all, this is your tenant's home. Make sure to ask your tenant if there is anything that needs to be repaired. This helps put your tenant at ease and shows them you have their best interests in mind and want to keep the home in good repair.

> **REAL STORIES: 24-HOUR NOTICE**
> Obviously, no one wants a stranger walking unannounced into their home. Therefore, it is common courtesy, as well as the law, to notify tenants in advance when we will be entering the home. The reason for entering the home is usually for routine maintenance. In this particular case, we had our automated call system notify tenants by phone that we would be changing their furnace filters the following day. Unbeknownst to us, one of our tenants, Will, had changed his phone number but had not notified us of the change. Naturally, we were using the phone numbers provided on the lease agreement form, so the automated notification meant for Will never made it to him.
>
> When our technician entered his property to change his furnace filter, therefore, Will was furious. He called us, threatening to sue. While the situation was unpleasant, at least we did not need to worry about being sued, at least not successfully sued. After all, Will had not notified us of his number change, and because we were using an automated voice calling system, we had on record that we had called his number on file and left a message.
>
> Lesson: Good systems protect you from lawsuits.

During the walk-through, you are trying to spot obvious areas of concern, not find the one outlet that does not work. At the same time, there is a delicate balance you must achieve. The Right to Quiet Enjoyment is a covenant that promises a tenant can possess the property in peace without disturbance with hostile claims. Basically this prevents you, the landlord, from coming onto the property without good reason. Coming on the property whenever you feel like it is not only potentially illegal, but is also simply bad ethics. With that said, keep your walk-through assessment brief and look for the following items:

- *General cleanliness of the property*
- *Smells that do not fit with a clean property*
- *Unauthorized pets*
- *Unauthorized smoking*
- *Unauthorized modifications to the property*
- *Make sure all smoke alarms are functional*
- *Damages in walls or doors covered up by posters*
- *Dripping faucets or running toilets that raise the water bill*
- *Exterior doors that do not seal, resulting in high heat and A/C bills*

Consistent walk-throughs will accomplish three important things:

1. Problem tenants are identified early, and the appropriate notices are sent in order to document any non-compliance events that take place in case an eviction becomes necessary or you end up in litigation.

2. Tenants understand that you are serious about maintaining the property, and you expect them to do the same.

3. Quarterly walk-throughs are a great way to identify maintenance items that need to be repaired. Unaddressed maintenance is one of the largest reasons for losing good tenants.

REAL STORIES: THE 4-LETTER WORD

We began managing a property we didn't realize had the potential for problems with the 4-letter word of rental properties: Mold. The basement had gotten wet before we managed it, and the owner had done only cosmetic repairs. The wet drywall had not been replaced, leaving a perfect environment for mold. We placed an excellent tenant in the property--he had a perfect credit history, he always paid on time, and he spent time improving the property, paying to replace carpet and have the house painted.

Soon after moving in, the tenant started feeling miserable. He called our property manager, James.

"I don't know what's going on," he said. "But ever since I've moved into this house, I have felt sick." He described his symptoms, and they were classic symptoms of someone reacting to mold.

James was upfront. "You may have mold in the house. I will get a mold test done."

The mold test came back positive. James had a mold remediation company get an estimate together for fixing the mold problem. He passed this information along to the owner. And then James made a mistake. The owner promised to take care of the problem immediately, but James did not follow up with the owner to make sure the mold had been eradicated. The owner, meanwhile, took no action.

Two months went by, and James received another call from the tenant. "This mold is still making me sick," he said.

Astonished that the owner had not fixed the problem, and horrified that the tenant had remained living in those conditions for two months, James immediately let the tenant out of his lease.

Never assume anything. Always follow up to ensure your standards and procedures are being followed.

FAILURE TO ACCOUNT FOR TENANT TURNOVER COSTS

Whenever a tenant leaves your property, you will assume several costs associated with finding a new tenant. Making your property rent-ready and finding another qualified tenant can be costly. The typical cost of a turnover is equal to three month's rent or more.

The costs of a turnover include:

1. **Property management fee.** Most property management companies charge a tenant placement or leasing fee equal to 50-100% of one month's rent to advertise and show the property, qualify a new tenant, and negotiate and sign a lease.

2. **The cost of vacancy.** As you read earlier, the cost of vacancy can be significant, especially when it is an unexpected cost. That is the key – unexpected cost. You've heard it said that failure to plan is planning to fail. If you don't plan or budget for the inevitable cost of vacancy, you may find you are unable to cover the mortgage, taxes, or other bills when they come due.

3. **The cost of making your property rent-ready.** The property in which you currently live likely has items that need to be repaired, cleaned, or organized; chances are, these items have needed attention for quite some time. So why is it that these details have never been addressed or resolved? Likely, you are simply procrastinating, have learned to ignore them, or have trivialized them as minor issues not worth your time. The same thing happens with rental properties and tenants.

Before new tenants move in, the property is probably in the best shape it will ever be during their tenancy, yet during the first month or two of tenancy, your renters will find the most problems. Our experience suggests when a property is new to tenants, they notice everything that doesn't work properly, isn't clean enough, etc. By months three and four, they tend to stop noticing little items, have learned to ignore them as trivial details, and have moved on with their normal daily routine. Why does this matter? Because the tenant who stays two or three years will have less maintenance requests than three tenants who each stay just one year. Also, with a long term tenant, a property investor saves time and money as he or she doesn't have to clean/replace carpet, paint, wash windows, or incur any of the other multitude of expenses associated with attracting a new tenant.

Turnover can be one of your biggest expenses, and as we've stated above, getting top dollar rent is not always the best strategy. Once a lease expires, the tenant will start looking at comparable rents and move as soon as they find something cheaper. Profitable investors know this, and they look at market rent prior to the end of the tenant's lease so as to determine whether the rental price should be increased or lowered. If market rents have dropped in the past year, consider offering the tenant a new lease at a lower price or offering them an incentive (such as free carpet cleaning) to encourage them to sign a new lease.

Consider the following example as a guide to the cost of turnover and the benefit of market rent research and incentives. If a $1,000 per month rental goes vacant, you may have to pay a $500-$1000 tenant placement or leasing fee, absorb the $1,000 cost of a vacant month, plus do some improvements, such as painting ($500-$1,000), to attract new tenants. The turnover could cost you $3,000. However, if you instead offer the incentive of decreasing the rent by $100/month, this only costs you $1,200 over the course of a year. As always, property and rental decisions must be based on numbers, not emotions, as this is one of the biggest differentiators between profitable and unprofitable real estate investors.

FAILURE TO PERFORM SIMPLE PREVENTIVE MAINTENANCE

Simple preventative maintenance performed on a regular basis pays big dividends over the course of time. From servicing the furnace before winter to changing furnace filters to fertilizing the lawn, these cost-effective measures can potentially save you thousands of dollars in major repairs. For example, one of the most simple, yet often neglected, items involves maintaining a property's gutters.

Gutters must be cleaned in the fall, because if they become clogged during the winter, ice dams may build and cause water damage to the roof and even the home's interior. In my personal home, I witnessed water leaking from the ceiling into the kitchen! With further investigation, I found a large ice dam on the roof covered with snow. When I put my hand under the snow, I discovered a hidden pool of water sitting on the roof.

Because the gutter was blocked with ice, this water could not escape and instead seeped under the shingles into the home's interior. This costly repair could have been avoided with the simple cleaning of the gutters during the prior fall.

Cleaning the leaves from the gutters, however, does not guarantee the home will not build ice dams. Weather conditions and how the home is heated and insulated also play a critical role. I have also seen down spouts "explode" from water being trapped in them, freezing, and expanding; this eventually causes the seams to burst. Cleaning gutters before winter will at least give the roof and gutters a fighting chance during a hard winter.

Gutters should also be cleaned in the spring but for a different reason. Plugged gutters cause rain water to run over the gutters and down beside the foundation, which can cause water to enter a property's basement. In addition to cleaning gutters, confirm that all down spouts are intact and unplugged. Most of the time, water can be kept out of a basement with well-maintained gutters and by making sure the landscape grade flows away from the foundation. If you own property in multiple states and climates, be aware of the unique maintenance challenges each present. For example, some states do not have basements, and some dry southern states have swamp coolers instead of air conditioners.

An ounce of prevention is worth a pound of cure. By making these property site maintenance tasks into habits, you will build a solid foundation for profitable investing by protecting your asset.

LACK OF GOOD RECORD KEEPING

Profitable real estate investment portfolios record and maintain massive amounts of information. Information includes but is not limited to leases, applications with proof of ID, tenant ledgers, contact information, unit details, maintenance records, assets at the property such as appliances, assessment reports, pictures, videos, and more.

Collection agencies and the courts struggle with collection efforts without proof of ID and information gathered on tenant applications.

> ### REAL STORIES: INSUFFICIENT TENANT RECORDS
> For example, after agreeing to manage several of Dillon's duplexes we realized he did not have sufficient records for us to even begin management. The documentation was so bad we had to resort to consulting tax records to find his properties. In one unit we found squatters.
> How do you evict a squatter? In order to file an eviction lawsuit, we needed the legal names of the people being evicted. After six months of legal battles, we finally received approval to have the building condemned by the city building code enforcement so that no one would be allowed to live in the property regardless of their name.

Keep in mind that each state follows its own eviction regulations.

In addition to accurate tenant records, property owners must keep accurate accounting records.

> **REAL STORIES: INSUFFICIENT ACCOUNTING RECORDS**
>
> Jaron came to us with 20 units and a bad case of heartburn. He said, "I feel like I am spinning circles. I can't keep up." Small wonder when we learned he had a full time job in addition to wearing all of the management team hats including, maintenance tech, bookkeeper, tax person, attorney, leasing manager, and more. Within two years of buying the properties he was facing foreclosure and bankruptcy.
>
> We helped him avoid bankruptcy and foreclosure on half the properties by providing good management and short selling several of the units. However, poor records made the process a bumpy ride. We found that two of the tenants had not paid rent for more than six months, and one of the tenants had not paid for more than a year. Jaron lost his properties and his retirement account largely because of poor record keeping, spreading himself too thin, and not understanding the consequences.

DISMISSING THE VALUE OF PETS

Pets! The thought brings varied reactions from different people. Tenants think of their pet as part of their family. A pet is something to be loved, enjoyed, and cared for. Many cannot think of parting with a family pet with which they have shared numerous fond memories. As the property owner, though, you may have a far different opinion. Your main thoughts will focus on pet-induced property damage, such as urine, vomit, and feces in the carpet along with scratches and bite marks on doors, walls, wood floors, and cabinets. In addition, you may worry about neighbor complaints regarding barking dogs, citations from the city because pet feces litter neighborhood lawns, or possibly ruined grass resulting from an animal's digging or running patterns. How can an animal bring out such varied reactions in people? It is a simple matter of risk vs. reward.

When pets are allowed into a rental property, your risks most definitely increase. The question is, does the reward also increase? We must remember that, as with any investment, owning rental property contains risk. **Without risk, there is no reward. So, the key is not to avoid risk, but to manage it.** We do this frequently with insurance. Holding a fire insurance policy does not mean our house won't burn down, but it does mean that if the house burns down, we will not be ruined financially. The same applies to renting to tenants with pets. All the precautions in the world will not keep tenants and pets from damaging a property, but the proper risk management will help pay for the damage if it occurs.

Collection agencies and the courts struggle with collection efforts without proof of ID and information gathered on tenant applications.

Even though there are risks associated with accepting pets, did you know that there is also risk in not accepting pets? After all, a large percentage of tenants own pets. If you, the property owner, are determined not to have pets in the property, you cut your property off from many otherwise qualified tenants. How does this affect you financially?

For argument's sake, let's assume that out of 100 applicants, 75 of them would qualify for your home based on credit, criminal, and previous landlord background checks. Let's further assume that 50 of the 75 qualified tenants have pets and 25 do not have pets. If you have a strict "No

Pet" policy, you will be competing with other no pet properties for the 25 non pet owning qualified tenants, while properties that accept pets will have 75 qualified tenants to choose from.

Remember that pet-friendly properties will accept tenants who do not own pets as well. If your property remains vacant for one month, you have lost real money that you will never be able to recover. That is the risk of not accepting pets. But, let's assume that you were able to rent your property to one of the 25 non pet owning tenants. Wonderful! But, why were you able to attract one of the 25 non pet owning tenants? In a free market, you must compete with others who are also in the market place. In order to compete and win, you have to offer a better product, with more benefits, at a lower cost to the customer. In rental terms, that means offering a more expensive property or one that includes more utilities in the rent for less rent than other similar properties that will and will not accept pets.

What about the properties that accept pets? They are also competing for tenants, but they have a larger pool of tenants to choose from and fewer properties competing for those tenants. Pet-friendly properties have access to all 75 qualified tenants. This means that the pet-friendly properties in our example are 3 times more likely to rent to a qualified tenant. Because they will accept pets, the pet-friendly properties have increased pet risk but less vacancy risk. If you are still unsure about the value of accepting pets and the amount of pet risk you are willing to assume, consider the following fundamental actions you can take to protect yourself.

Pet-Friendly Homes Are 3 Times More Likely To Be Rented

100 APPLICANTS

50 QUALIFIED WITH PET

25 QUALIFIED WITH NO PET

Pet-Friendly Homes = 75 Qualified Tenants
Non-Pet Homes = 25 Qualified Tenants

1. Hire a professional property manager. Property managers implement systems to ensure the right steps are taken and followed up on when managing a tenant with pets. This is a great way to limit your pet risk. The property manager will most likely take care of all the following details.

2. Charge an extra pet deposit and/or pet rent. Believe it or not, pet owners expect to pay extra for having pets in a rental.

3. Conduct thorough credit/criminal background checks and landlord references. These will help you determine if the tenant is a good risk. Individuals who pay their bills, are not in trouble with the law, and have no collection agencies pursuing them tend to be responsible in many areas of their life. These individuals also frequently make the most responsible pet owners and are most likely to pay for any pet related property damage.

4. Place limits on the number, type, and size of pets allowed. You may put any limit you like on the property. Some examples are: No aggressive breeds, dogs under 25lbs, no cats, animals must be spayed/neutered/declawed, two pet maximum, etc.

5. Add a pet addendum, which addresses the special requirements and responsibilities of owning a pet in the property.

6. Check with your insurance company to see how pet damages are handled.

7. Have a pet policy/handbook. Know your limits in advance, and make sure the tenants also know those limits. Having clear boundaries is a good way to hold tenants accountable.

8. Conduct regular assessments. Nothing is more important for spotting problems early and putting your mind at ease than getting eyes inside the property to see for yourself.

Let's assume the worst happens and a pet(s) damages your $1,000/month rental property. How much is really at risk? Because you accepted pets, you lowered your vacancy risk by a minimum of one month, which is equivalent to at least $1,000. There were two pets in this property, and you collected $25/month per pet, which equals $600/year. In addition, you collected a $1,000 damage security deposit (not related to pets). Thus, you will have $2,600 to help pay for pet damage. However, if there is no damage, you will have made an extra $1,600 over the course of a year by renting to a tenant with pets.

You have increased your annual return by 13% by accepting pets if they do not damage the property. If the damage is $2,600, you will have a zero net gain. If the damage is more than $2,600, you will have a loss. However, you will only suffer that loss if your property insurance does not cover the damage and you cannot get the tenant to pay for the damage. You will need to decide if the risk of accepting pets is worth the reward of accepting pets.

FAILURE TO UNDERSTAND AND FOLLOW OCCUPANCY RULES

Some states and cities have adopted a "maximum number of occupants ordinance" for rental property. You will need to check with your specific state or city, but in some jurisdictions, the ordinance says that no more than three unrelated people can inhabit a rental property. "Unrelated people" means people who are more distantly related than cousins. For example, these ordinances would not allow four college roommates to live in the same property, but a family consisting of a grandpa, father, mother, uncle, two children, and a cousin could live in the same rental property. Another allowable combination is a family of four people together with two completely unrelated people. While the total number of occupants is six, the family of four only counts as "one" person.

Some landlords think, "This occupancy ordinance rules are unenforced, so why bother following them?" We can tell you from experience that jurisdictions are following up on these ordinances. Enforcement usually arises from a neighbor's complaint about too much coming and going at the property. Consider renting a four bedroom house to four or five college students. Each of those students has a car, a girlfriend or boyfriend, and about six other friends or classmates who will come over to study, visit, or hangout. What starts out as four to five cars can quickly turn into ten to fifteen cars and a lot of activity. This does not mean that there is a party going on, loud music, or any other sort of disruption. It does mean that a residential street is packed with vehicles. At this point the landlord will get a call from the city wondering how many unrelated people are on the lease. If the landlord has signed the lease with more than three unrelated people, there will be consequences because the lease violates the city ordinance. However, the lease itself is a legally binding contract giving the right of occupancy to the tenants.

If you find yourself in this situation, immediately contact an attorney if you don't already have one on your team (which you should). Better yet, keep the law, and don't involve yourself in this situation in the first place.

Guidelines for Occupancy Rules

Property managers and landlords need to be aware of all practical occupancy considerations in their local community. If you are an investor, ask yourself the tough questions in advance before the city asks you these questions. For example, how many people should you allow to live in the property? A good rule of thumb is no more than two people per bedroom plus one more. The "plus one more" can sleep in the living room on the sofa.

Also, depending upon your city's occupancy ordinances consider the ages and genders of the occupants. While you need to be careful not to discriminate based on age and gender, you should consider adopting a policy that allows families to split up boys and girls in separate bedrooms above a certain age. For example, a family of five with a mom, dad, and two girls and a boy all above the age of twelve, should rent at minimum a three-bedroom home, even though they would fit in a two-bedroom rental.

These are the small details that can cause big problems in the long run if they are not dealt with right away. As the old saying goes, "Never put off tomorrow what you can get done today;" in property management, those details put off today can become tomorrow's litigation.

FAILURE TO ANTICIPATE POTENTIAL PROBLEMS

Many obstacles stand between you and the success of your rental properties. Understanding these potential problems in advance, however, will increase your success rate and ultimately your profits.

To fully understand this concept, consider marathon runners and what they refer to as "The Wall." "The Wall" happens sometime between miles 17 and 20. When runners hit "The Wall", their muscles hurt, it becomes hard to breath, and their body feels like it is shutting down. This experience is shared by all marathon runners, but without proper knowledge of and preparation for how to handle "The Wall," it is easy to give up because they feel as if something is seriously wrong. However, if these runners understand what happens when they hit "The Wall" and are prepared in advance to handle it, they will be equipped and trained to push through. Understanding that an obstacle is ahead and training in advance for it means the difference between quitting at mile 18 or victory in finishing.

Prepare in advance for the following obstacles in the same way as a marathon runner prepares for "The Wall" – expect them and plan ahead. Although you may feel overwhelmed at times, understand the situation you are in and train to push through for your strong finish and success.

REAL STORIES: FURNITURE FIGHT

Max approached us to manage his property, a house that he was vacating for various reasons (divorce, losing business, starting college). Initially, everything seemed fine, other than one thing: the house was still full of Max's furniture, and Max didn't want the furniture.

"Could I leave it in the house?" he asked our property manager. "Perhaps the renters could use it?"

Having encountered so many orange couches, torn cushions, and broken chair legs, the property manager stifled the urge to roll his eyes. However, upon examination, he realized that the furniture was up-to-date, clean, and free of defects. A few days later, he had an approved tenant who was ready to move in, and he told Max he would offer this option to the tenants.

"Great!" said Max. "Tell them they don't even need to pay me an extra fee for the furnishings. I'm just so happy I don't need to find storage for it."

The tenants accepted the offer gladly, and everyone seemed happy. Max seemed like a great guy, and the tenants wouldn't need to buy new furniture. There was just one small detail overlooked: the Lease Agreement was not edited to reflect the furniture agreement.

Unfortunately, small details can become big details. Several months after the tenant moved into Max's house, Max called us. His voice over the phone was cheerful.

"Hi!" he said. "Remember that furniture in my house? Well, I found a buyer for it and I'd like you to inform the tenant I'll be stopping by to pick it up next Monday."

Our property manager was nonplussed. "But you can't just take the furniture," he reasoned. "You told the tenants they could use it."

But Max was insistent. He had found a buyer, he could use the extra cash, and he was going to get that furniture. Our property manager called the tenant and explained the situation to him. The tenant was every bit as adamant as Max.

"I was told I could use the furniture, and I am going to use it," he insisted.

Our property manager was stuck. The agreement was not in writing; therefore, he could not effectively end the matter. All he could do was attempt to mediate. But Max and the tenant were not open to mediation. The situation escalated. Max threatened to enter the house without the tenant's permission and take the furniture. The tenant, in turn, threatened: "I'll call the police if he enters my home. And if that fails," he said ominously, "I have an AR-15 rifle."

Eventually, Max gathered a large posse of his buddies and arrived at the tenant's home with a trailer. When he arrived, he realized that the tenant had had the same idea; five of HIS buddies stood just inside the entryway, their arms crossed.

Thankfully, no confrontation actually occurred. Max wisely remained in the yard while his friends entered the house and dragged the furniture out. The tenant, in turn, restrained from flashing his AR-15, and Max and his friends drove away with the furniture.

Several days later, Max realized a cushion was missing from his couch. Apparently not content that he had got away from that place with both his life AND 99.9% of his furniture, he was determined to go back to the house and get that one missing cushion. At this point, the tenant, understandably at his wits end, put an alarm system in the house, and Max, apparently gaining some perspective with the passage of time, decided against retrieving the missing cushion.

We learned a lesson. The situation could have been nipped in the bud if only the furniture agreement had been written in the contract. Never, never, NEVER think that a verbal agreement and seeming goodwill is sufficient. Always put agreements in writing.

FAILURE TO AVOID POTENTIAL LAWSUITS

Rental properties are potential mine fields for lawsuits if you are uneducated and ill-prepared. Before investing, consider the following possible legal issues:

Fair housing issues such as:

- *steering*
- *discriminatory advertising*

Discriminatory leasing practices based on or against things such as:

- *Familial status*
- *Single mothers with children*
- *Companion pets*
- *People with disabilities*

Habitability issues such as:

- *Not supplying water, heat, or electric when required*
- *Not performing maintenance when required*
- *Properly handling security deposits and refunds*
- *Property hazards*
- *Mold*
- *Water in the basement*
- *Lead Based Paint*
- *Asbestos*

These are all potential problems with rental units, and how you address the above items will determine whether or not you will end up in court.

IGNORING SMALL LEGAL DETAILS THAT LEAD TO BIG PROBLEMS

- Not returning a security deposit in a time frame prescribed by law
- Discrimination or fair housing violations
- Not handling environmental hazards appropriately or in a timely manner
- Habitability issues (tenant claims your property unsuitable to live in)
- Retaliation against a tenant
- Not following the correct eviction procedure

NOT DEALING ADEQUATELY WITH COMPLAINTS

You will have tenant disputes and complaints. Regardless if they are legit or not, you will have to spend time dealing with them. In addition, if the neighbors complain, you will also have to call them back and explain how the situation is being handled.

Occasionally, tenants will have a health inspection done on their unit *without your consent.* If you have anything that isn't working properly, you will be notified and given a deadline by which to remedy any issue. If the deadline passes and everything doesn't meet city standard, the unit can be declared uninhabitable, the tenant can be forced to move out, and no one can occupy the unit until the changes are made.

How Can a Good Investment Go Bad?

MISTAKE 1

TIME. Your real estate investment will take time. Your time. You will need to conduct showings, take care of make-ready maintenance, and handle tenant calls (on the weekends, after hours, on holidays, and when you are on vacation). You will run the risk of potentially decreasing productivity from your day job. You must make enough money from your rental to pay yourself a wage for the time you will spend managing the property. Remember: your time is not free. When your tenant's day-job ends, his or her questions and problems begin.

MISTAKE 2

INEXPERIENCE. When it comes to rental properties, you will always be faced with something new. Inexperience in business, especially real estate, is expensive. You absolutely can learn, but it will take time and cost you money. Two main ingredients will help solve this problem: Experience and time. Of course you will make mistakes, but today's mistakes will become tomorrow's opportunities for more profit, if you decide to learn! The most successful people in real estate are the people who refused to quit and worked hard.

MISTAKE 3

EXPECTATIONS. Just as in any relationship, miscommunicated expectations are the root cause of many arguments. Set clear expectations from the beginning with your tenant. Then get it in writing. There will be times of uncertainty, but if you have proper documentation, most misunderstandings can be resolved. There is absolutely no substitute for a well-written lease agreement, a lesson we unfortunately learned the hard way during our early days of property management.

MISTAKE 4

NUMBERS. Success and Failure rise and fall on numbers. The strategy of waiting till the end of the year to see if you made money might have worked in years past, but no longer. Your investment might be dead by the end of the year. Knowing your numbers will help you make accurate and educated course corrections along the way.

CHAPTER 4
The Cost of Overlooked Details

What are the primary legal necessities that are often overlooked? From our experience, when we have assumed a lease from another landlord, we often see small legal details missed that can cost big dollars down the road. In truth, any legal detail missed, big or small, has the potential to cost you money. Some of the most common mistakes include: not listing the exact amount of the security deposit, forgetting to place an expiration date on the lease, and failing to name each occupant who has the right to live in the property. Of course, there are many other areas of concern on which your legal team will provide counsel, but start with the items below and work your way out.

NO WRITTEN LEASE

Even though verbal leases have legal ramifications, you still must have a written lease signed by you and your tenant. Without upfront clear expectations, there are countless ways to get in trouble such as late rent payments, damages from departing tenants or repairs to name a few. Not only do we have short memories, but when we do remember things, we have a strong tendency to skew our memories in our favor.

RENTING TO SOMEONE FACING BANKRUPTCY

If you are renting to someone going into bankruptcy, (i.e. before the bankruptcy is discharged), you must get permission from the Federal bankruptcy judge before you can collect rent from them. This poses obvious problems, so I strongly suggest you avoid this path altogether. Don't try to be the hero; go find another tenant! If they declare bankruptcy while renting from you, contact an attorney immediately. You do not want to irritate a Federal judge by initiating collections or eviction proceedings.

WHEN TENANCY ENDS, LITIGATION BEGINS

Litigation can take several forms, and you can be left to handle many legal ramifications if you enter this situation with any vulnerabilities. One of the most common legal problems is a dispute over the security deposit.

For example, if the tenant has damaged the carpets, how much can you charge them for the repair? The tenant will often claim the carpet was damaged or dirty when they moved in. How are you going to prove that it was clean and in good condition? The answer to this is a system. Create a system for handling this situation. With a system to follow, you can avoid reacting out of emotion and take effective action despite the inevitable drama of the situation.

To begin creating a system, consider that many things can be used in court as evidence. You can use pictures, video footage, written contracts, and detailed move-in inspection lists that you and the tenant sign. Have a document filing system in printed form with digital copies backed up in multiple locations so you absolutely know you can get quick access to this information under almost any circumstance.

ONE TENANT REMAINING, ONE TENANT LEAVING

Sometimes tenants move in and out on a rolling basis. This frequently happens with college roommates where the property is rented to three or more people. Typically, within six months of the lease beginning, one of the roommates leaves, and a new tenant takes his or her place. The breakup of romantic partners will often create a similar situation. Who are the responsible parties on the lease? Who is supposed to receive the security deposit now when the lease ends? Don't leave room for these small mistakes to haunt you when

Don't leave room for small mistakes to haunt you when the lease expires. Set clear expectations, and record every transaction and financial detail.

the lease expires. Set clear expectations, record every transaction and financial detail as it relates to each tenant, and take every precaution to protect yourself.

PROPERTY SALE

What happens when you sell a property? Should you give the deposit to the new owner? Not unless the tenant gives his or her okay. In a worst-case scenario, the new owner might spend the deposit, and the tenant will come back and ask you for it since you were the "escrow agent" to whom they originally gave the deposit.

TENANT AND LANDLORD LAWS

Become very familiar with the following laws and regulations:

- Habitability Guidelines
- Landlord/Tenant Law
- Fair Housing Act (see below for further description)

Violation of these laws and regulations will ultimately result in a visit to the judge. Courts in most states will side with the tenant against the landlord, so avoid going to court through legal understanding and documentation. Why does the judge side with the tenant by default? The main reason stems from the landlord's responsibility to offer the terms of the lease. If you write the lease and there is a dispute over the understanding of the lease, the court will judge in favor of the tenant because it was the landlord's responsibility to clearly communicate the terms of the lease.

On the other hand, if you break habitability laws, then the tenant may be able to legally break the lease, leaving you with vacancy costs. Conversely, instead of vacating the property, the tenant can instead fix the problem on their own and subtract the repair expense from the rent. Bottom line, understand the law or have team members with a high legal understanding.

HABITABILITY GUIDELINES

Tenants expect their rental to be in a livable condition. For example, tenants can reasonably expect the roof not to leak, the furnace to provide heat, the plumbing system to provide fresh water, and the drain system to remove waste. Depending upon the lease agreement, habitability rules might require the landlord to supply water, fuel, and electric. For example, if the lease says that the landlord pays for the water and the city shuts off the water to the property for nonpayment, the landlord has made the property uninhabitable and the tenant may be able to lawfully break the lease and move out.

LANDLORD/TENANT LAW

States have adopted their own Landlord/Tenant Laws and they are often part of the states' codified laws. This set of laws, govern the interactions between landlords, rental agents, and tenants. For example, contained in your state's Landlord/Tenant Law you are likely to find the laws relating to the security deposit, i.e. the maximum allowed to be collected, how the interest must be handled, what type of bank account must be used, how a claim against the security deposit is to be filed, how much time the landlord has to return the deposit, and the penalties for not doing so.

FAIR HOUSING ACT

The Fair Housing Act is part of the Civil Rights Act of 1968. Congress passed this act and several other laws in order to solve the problem of unlawful discrimination in residential housing based on color, race, sex, nationality, or religion. The act is great for civil rights, but it can create a potential problem in terms of your rental unit.

Fair Housing has the potential to be a serious problem because it leaves you vulnerable to legal attacks. For example, you may have a one-bedroom apartment and seek to rent it to a single person with no children. Even inserting vocabulary into the lease agreement that states only one person can occupy the unit may cause legal problems. If you turn down a single mother and her daughter, it could appear you are discriminating, which could invite investigation and fines by HUD (US Department of Housing and Urban Development).

These laws have changed over the years while at the same time Fair Housing regulations have become more strict in how they are defined and enforced. Federal Fair Housing laws cover all states, and some states have additional protected classes. Real Estate and Multi-Housing Associations often offer Fair Housing regulation training for a modest fee.

While most landlords understand they cannot discriminate based upon class status, there are also other items you must be prepared to handle, such as granting disabled tenants accommodations and reasonable modifications to the property. You must know the laws on service animals. If you have a "no pet" policy, you must be prepared for the tenant who has a service animal (such as a Seeing Eye Dog). In addition, doctors are starting to "prescribe" pets for people with depression and other mental disorders. If you refuse to rent to someone who owns a companion pet for a health disorder, you might inadvertently be discriminating and violating state or federal law.

Fair Housing impacts your entire business, from how you advertise and answer the phone to how you treat prospective tenants and current tenants when you meet them at the property. An investigation, lawsuit, and/or fines will certainly (and most likely negatively) impact your return on investment in significant ways.

INSURANCE REQUIREMENTS

Insuring your rental property or properties is not an option. Liability and property damage coverage are the two cornerstones for insuring your property. Liability covers you in the event an individual is injured at the property. Property damage insures circumstances such as fire, hail, etc. According to your region, you may have additional specific coverage such as flood, tornado, hurricane, etc.

Some insurance companies require the tenant to carry renter's insurance while others do not. Generally, the landlord does not have to cover the tenant's property, but to make absolutely certain, it is a good idea to make renter's insurance a requirement for your tenants. For example, if the property burns down, the landlord's property insurance will cover the structure, and the renter's insurance will cover the tenant's personal property. I also highly recommend educating yourself about rent replacement insurance. If the fire destroys the property, the insurance company will pay the rent for the remainder of the lease.

> **Insuring your rental property or properties is not an option.**

Some things to watch for on your policy are vacancy details, making sure the policy is for non-owner occupied and also what can happen during vacancy. For example, some insurance policies only cover a water leak for 30 days of vacancy. If the property is vacant longer than 30 days and you have a water leak you will end up paying out of pocket.

Insurance is a way to pass the risk on to someone else for a price. You need to have enough to protect yourself, but not so much that you are insurance-poor. The key is to manage the risk but not eliminate the risk. If you eliminate the risk, you will also eliminate your profit. Remember, there is no profit without risk. You can't expect someone else to assume all the risk while you make a profit. You have to find the balance.

Legal Documents

- Lease agreement
- Pet addendum
- Mold addendum
- Lead-based paint addendum and HUD brochure (Required by law for an older property)
- Addendums required by state or local regulatory agencies
- City rental permit and inspection
- Early lease termination agreement
- Security deposit documentation
- Transfer of security deposit receipt
- Eviction process and documentation
- General release (used when you have a dispute with a tenant and have come to a settlement)
- 3-Day notice to pay or quit (may be called something different by state)
- Security deposit claim document
- Pool addendum
- Other addendums (anything that is unique to the property, i.e. tree house, gardens, pond, outbuildings, special floors, etc.)
- Lease violation letter

Processes

- Prospective tenant application
- Process for tenant vacancy
- Process for tenant leaving early
- Move-in and move-out inspection list (I suggest making a video as well)
- Maintenance processes and standards
- Accounting processes (i.e. collecting and recording rents, late fees, bounced checks, refunds, bills, liabilities (such as security deposits), etc.)
- Process for document storage and retrieval
- Process for tenant on-boarding
- Process for entering a property after giving notice.
- Policy for entering a property when only minors are home.
- Process for late rent collection, serving legal notices, and processing evictions

Remember

Litigation begins when tenancy ends, and the judge will tend to favor the tenant. Protect yourself, your family, and your investment.

CHAPTER 5

Maintenance Secrets that $ave

I once heard an auto mechanic mention that one of the best ways to insure the longevity of your vehicle is to consistently perform simple maintenance procedures such as changing the oil. This "pay now or pay later" attitude definitely applies to your rental property. By consistently performing basic maintenance procedures you can avoid expensive repairs over the lifetime of your investment. The following maintenance procedures are ones that should be on every property maintenance checklist.

CLEAN GUTTERS

Gutters need cleaning once in the fall and once in the spring. If they get plugged during the winter, ice dams can build up and cause water damage to the roof and even the interior of the home. I've seen some homes with water leaking into them because of an ice dam.

Plugged gutters in the spring will cause water to run over the gutter, down the foundation of the house, and potentially into the basement. In addition to cleaning gutters, make sure all down spouts are intact and unplugged. Most of the time water can be kept out of a basement by having well maintained gutters and by making sure the grading of the landscaping flows away from the foundation.

CLEAN OUTSIDE A/C COMPRESSOR UNIT

Add this to your spring checklist. Regularly cleaning your A/C unit ensures the machine is cooling and running optimally. Over the entire year, various debris can clog the cooling fins. A dirt-filled fan blower, low coolant levels, and other small issues will not only reduce the effectiveness of your unit, but also wear it out over time forcing you to invest more capital into the maintenance of your property. This entire task can take less than 2 hours to complete and save you hundreds of dollars in the process.

SERVICE THE HEATING SYSTEM

With maintenance, you can pay now or later. This applies directly to your heating system as well as everything else on this list. You need to check the system at least once annually to ensure optimal functioning and a long lifetime out of your home equipment.

REGULARLY CHANGE FURNACE FILTERS

A majority of your repair calls will relate to problems caused by irregular replacement of the furnace filter. Changing the furnace filters on a regular basis is a very effective preventative maintenance habit. During the summer, handle problems with the filter and A/C unit before they begin. Otherwise, your tenants will call on their days off (usually evenings and weekends), disrupting your summer schedule.

HAVE AN A/C OR FURNACE SOLUTION CHECKLIST

Create a checklist for tenants to walk through before calling you or the HVAC company. This prevents unnecessary service calls and also helps determine the problem in an efficient manner. Include the following on your checklist:

- *Is the filter clean?*
- *Is the thermostat set correctly?*
- *Are there fresh batteries in the thermostat?*
- *Has the switch beside the furnace or A/C been accidentally switched off?*
- *Has a fuse or breaker been tripped in the fuse box?*

INSTALL CARPET WITHOUT A PAD IN YOUR BASEMENT

Installing carpet without padding has multiple benefits. If water gets into the basement, it is much easier to dry the floor and carpet if there is no padding. If you are handling the maintenance, this means less time on the job for you, and if you are hiring a company, you will spend less money. Mold and mildew will have a difficult time growing in a basement without the padding. If you have a pad in the basement and it gets wet, there is really no way to dry it before mold starts to grow. You must rip out the pad, dry the carpet, and then install a new pad. Depending upon the type of water infiltration and contamination, you may or may not be able to salvage the carpet.

HAVE A WEED AND FEED LAWN PROGRAM

Curb appeal is critical to selling or renting a home and giving tenants a quality experience. Have a strategic, scheduled plan for your lawn. They don't need to be the best lawns in the neighborhood, but they do need to blend in with the neighborhood at the very least. Schedule a regular time for mowing, fertilizing, and watering to assure the lawn looks optimal.

FIX SMALL PROBLEMS BEFORE THEY BECOME BIG PROBLEMS

Big problems both in life and with your rental property are best avoided by paying attention to small details. Water in the basement is a big problem that can be prevented by doing small things such as cleaning the gutters and making sure the grading of the landscape flows away from the foundation. It's like getting a crack in your windshield. It starts out small, but before you know it, you have one big crack across your window. Focus on controlling and containing the smaller problems, and you will also prevent the larger ones from happening.

CHOOSE FUNCTIONAL EQUIPMENT AS OPPOSED TO FANCY EQUIPMENT

Forget about how equipment looks and focus on how well it works. Consider getting a used direct drive Whirlpool washing machine that can be repaired with readily accessible parts as opposed to a new model that costs more to fix than to replace. There is no need to buy all new equipment. Put in a little extra effort upfront to find slightly used equipment, and you will save money in the long run.

CONDUCT REGULAR MAINTENANCE ASSESSMENTS

Assessments are time consuming but necessary for your rental investment and will mitigate property damage. Quarterly assessments will help protect your investment. This does not mean a drive-by visitation but a thorough walk through of the entire property. Consider conducting assessments during: move-ins, move-outs, and when law-enforcement is called to the property.

USE THE SAME PAINT, BRAND COLOR, AND SHEEN

If you have multiple properties, this will save you money and time with less visits to the store and less details to manage for each property. You will be surprised how long it takes to figure out what color the paint is for a particular property, have it mixed, and then do the same process with different colors for different properties. Systemize everything you can for your rentals, including paint colors.

FIX WATER LEAKS RIGHT AWAY

If your water bill spikes unexpectedly, you may have a water leak. During your regular inspections, pay attention to the toilets, showerheads, outdoor/indoor faucets, and protect your outdoor spigots from freezing. Always track your water bill amount so you can gauge when the water bill is going up or spiking from the typical monthly cost.

Every athlete has glory-filled dreams of performing in front of millions of fans as they compete on their favorite professional team but few direct that passion to the day-to-day grind that involves no fans, no cheers and tons of hard work. The athletes that commit themselves to the grind also commit themselves to the greatness that accompanies it. Your rental property success demands the same attention to the small details and unglamorous work that will be required of you, if you are not working with a property manager, in order to succeed. Basic maintenance procedures will never fill you with excitement but they will help you achieve greatness. Commit to these basics and profits will follow.

CHAPTER 6
Insider Secrets for Maximizing Your Investment

Every industry carries with it secrets, or shortcuts if you will, that empower you to leverage the experience and pain of others in order to reach your goals faster while mitigating as much risk as possible. Your ability to ask for, receive and apply council from experienced investors will be in exact proportion to your level of profits. The points below are my attempt to list a few of those secrets I have witnessed and learned while watching many investors rise and fall.

SPEND MONEY ON ADVERTISING TO LIMIT VACANCY

Essentially, what you are selling is time. You must realize your time is a valuable asset that other people are willing to purchase from you; it would be a detrimental flaw on your part to give your time out for free. As the saying goes "Time is money," and when you train your mind to think this way, then we can begin discussing how to maximize profit from your rental property.

When you consider property vacancy, you need to realize that vacancy is actually theft – time theft. Every single day your rental property sits empty, a shoplifter by the name of "Vacancy" is stealing goods from your business. You must accept that this theft exists, and you must understand how to fight against it.

The theft of time will attack in a number of different ways, but the first is an empty property that just sits there eating up your money. In other words, you don't have a tenant. The only solution to fight against a true vacancy is to rent the property to the right tenant as quickly as possible. The question you must ask yourself is, "How can I get my property rented to the right tenants faster?"

Just as businesses spend money to protect their property from theft, so too must landlords spend money to reduce vacancies, or time theft. The Bottom Line: It is better to spend a large amount of money for a short period of time than a small amount for a longer period of time.

For example, you could either spend $200 on one month of advertising or $50 for 2 months. In order to make the best decision, you must calculate the cost of vacancy into both the costs and the time frame of your advertising campaign. Let's say you are renting out a property for $1,000.00 per month. If you spend $200.00 on advertising for 1 month, the actual cost is $1,200.00 (1 month vacancy plus advertising). If you opt for spending less and choose the "cheaper" $50 option, it might actually cost you $2,050.00 (2 month's vacancy plus advertising). There is a point where more advertising has a diminishing rate of return. However, when in doubt, opt for more advertising, not less.

Investing in good advertising can also reduce other types of rental theft, such as an economic vacancy and tenant damage. Simply getting your property rented is not a win in and of itself. What matters most is finding the right people. When you fill your property with a tenant that doesn't have capacity to pay, you have what is called an economic vacancy. An economic vacancy is where the tenant is physically occupying the property, but is late paying or can't pay for a period of time. Proper advertising helps limit this theft by increasing the likelihood of placing a good quality tenant in your unit. Good advertising increases demand for the rental and thus increases the pool of applicants. This allows you to hand-select the most financially responsible tenant for the unit instead of accepting a mediocre applicant who may end up not paying you.

> **When in doubt, opt for more advertising, not less.**

Limiting vacancy can also make the difference between a profitable return on investment (ROI) and a negative ROI. For example, an investor purchases a $150,000 single family home and finances it with 20% down. In this case, the investment is $30,000. If the investor wants to see an 8% annual positive cash flow, he would expect an annual ROI of $2,400 ($2,400/$30,000 = 8%). If the market rent for the property is $1,600, the investor would receive a 0% annual ROI if the property was vacant for 1.5 months. In other words, the difference between a profitable investment and an unprofitable investment can be as little as a month and a half of vacancy. Those 45 days on the market pass by very quickly.

PRICE LOW, RENT HIGH

People have an emotional response to money. They love it, want it, and fear losing it. Often markets are described in the terms of fear and greed. Price is not an objective value of the item. Rather, price is the perceived value placed upon an item by a subjective person. We can also think of markets in terms of scarcity and abundance, or supply and demand.

There are many times when we do irrational things with our money. For example, how many of us have bought the 1 gallon pail of ice cream because it is cheaper per ounce than the 1/2 gallon box of ice cream, only to have the gallon of ice cream crystalize in the freezer because we didn't eat it fast enough? In the end, we spend more money per ounce of ice cream consumed by buying the 1 gallon vs. the 1/2 gallon. This is just a simple example, but if we took the time to examine the economic decision we make on a daily basis because of the emotions of fear and greed, we would be shocked by how emotionally flawed our money decisions really are. Consider coupons, Buy One Get One Free, Loyalty cards, sales, rebates, 10 for $10, etc. All these gimmicks are not meant to save the consumer money. They are carefully planned strategies to get the consumer to buy more. With that said, how can a property investor use human emotion in their favor without being manipulative? First, we must understand what the emotions are and how to work with them.

Greed: This involves both tenant greed and investor greed. Often, investor greed takes the form of consciously over-pricing the rental. Investors begin thinking about how much *more* money they would make *if* they could just get the tenant to pay $100, $150, or $200 more per month. The prospect of making more money will eventually end up impacting their market perspective and will affect their decisions.

Tenant greed takes the form of finding a good deal. Tenant greed is the emotion that rental scammers use to fool their victims. By grossly underpricing a scammed property, the scammer preys upon the irrational greed of the tenant. The tenant will do ir-

> *If we took the time to examine the economic decision we make on a daily basis, we would be shocked by how emotionally flawed our money decisions are.*

rational things such as giving the scammer their bank account information or even sending the scammer a money order because they don't want someone else to grab this "awesome deal" before they do. They come to find their emotions have led them into the scammer's trap.

CAVEAT EMPTOR: BUYER BEWARE
One of our leasing agents, Don, showed a prospective tenant an upscale rental home, listed at $1400/mo. The leasing agent could detect only lukewarm interest. The prospective tenant seemed to like the property, but was noncommittal. It was Friday afternoon and was the last property he was showing for the day. At the end of the showing, he wished her a nice weekend and walked to his car, expecting to never hear from her again.

The weekend proceeded peacefully, but first thing the following Monday morning, Don's phone rang urgently. He was surprised when he realized it was this same person. However, she wasn't asking questions about the property. She had been scammed over the weekend and was distraught. She had gone home after viewing the house and spent some time browsing Craigslist for more rental options. She had come across the same house Don had just shown her. The pictures, the description, everything was the same--everything, that is, except the price. The price was $900/mo., $500 less than Don had it listed for.

She had truly liked what she saw during her walkthrough, but hadn't been able to afford the price. When she saw the killer deal on Craigslist, she fell for it instantly. She emailed the "owner," received a prompt reply, and immediately provided him with all the information he was after: social security number, bank account information, name, address--everything. Over the weekend, her bank account was hit four times. Thankfully, the bank shut down her account due to the suspicious activity, and she did not lose all the money in her account. But she did lose some money, and it was certainly a rattling experience.

When the emotion of greed causes a landlord to overprice a rental, they short circuit the tenant's emotion of greed, and the tenant's greed will opt for a similar property that has a lower price. As time goes on and more tenants pass on the overpriced property, the tenant emotions will turn to fear because of the length of time on the market. The property takes on a perceived stigma. Potential tenants will ask and wonder why nobody has rented the property for so long. They will build assumptions in their mind that will create confusion, and a confused mind always says no.

> **They will build assumptions in their mind that will create confusion, and a confused mind always says no.**

Now, the investor has not only lost the opportunity to use a tenant's greed to make a buying decision, but they now have an uphill battle to overcome any other potential tenant's fear of renting an undesirable property. In order to overcome tenant fear and again activate tenant greed, the property will truly have to be too good to pass up. However, this means that the price will have to be discounted far below the market value in order to attract a tenant.

The sweet spot is to price the rental slightly below the market at the time you list the property. The successful investor will have to control their own greed so they can capitalize on the greed of the tenant. With the property newly on the market and slightly underpriced, the prospective tenant thinks it is a good deal and decides to grab the rental before someone else does. Because the property rents quickly, vacancy theft is minimized. Because the property is seen as desirable, the investor is not left with a stigmatized property that must be rented at a steep discount.

KNOW YOUR NUMBERS

Profitable investors understand their money is made when they acquire a property, not afterwards. Therefore, they do their research and due diligence before investing. Even the best property manager or the best business plan in the world will never be able to compensate for a poor buying decision.

> *If purchased properly, a rental investment can make you money for years to come.*

If purchased properly, a rental investment can make you money for years to come. On the other hand, if the property has been purchased hastily and without due diligence, then it will be a constant source of frustration and disappointment. You will end up blaming the market, your tenants, and your property manager when in reality the purchase price will be at fault. What we see frequently happen in the real estate and rental market is paying too much for a property from the very beginning. As with all investments, we are only speculating on the future. The biggest problem that remains is that we don't know the future.

Real estate is a long-term investment strategy. The very act of buying and selling real estate is costly. The longer you are able to hold a property, the more likely it will be profitable.

Sometimes, people will rent out a property, not because it is a good investment, but because they cannot afford to sell the property at the current market price. In this case, the owner needs to temper their expectation. The goal of this type of situation is to stop the bleeding, at least until the sales market rebounds enough so they can sell at a profit instead of a loss. In this case, the owner might lose a few dollars each month, but this is preferable to having to short sale the property or let it go into foreclosure.

> *As an investor, you must anticipate the future with realistic expectations, a knowledgeable education, and the right questions.*

As an investor, you must anticipate the future with realistic expectations, a knowledgeable education, and the right questions. What sort of expenses can you expect this year? What sort of maintenance will need to be performed? Have you budgeted enough to cover all expenses?

You must also understand your goals. Is your strategy based on cash flow or equity? If the property has been heavily financed with little down, you will most likely need to focus on building equity. If you paid cash for the property, then you can focus directly on cash flow. Often, you cannot do both.

Most of these secrets revolve around money and clarity. If you have both, few things can stop you. If you are missing one of these two secrets, no amount of the other will matter much. Take these secrets and make them habits - habits of thought and action. Your vision will help you determine where to go and your habits will get you there.

CHAPTER 7
Questions for Qualifying a Property Manager

You are making the right choice by deciding to hire a property manager – there is no doubt. This will save you time, allow you to keep enjoying your lifestyle and give you a much greater chance of success with your rental unit.

But how do you find the right property manager? This is another decision and key hire to your real estate team and will definitely impact your return on investment in a positive or negative way, depending on the manager you hire. However you research this decision, here are some key questions you ask your potential manager before making your decision.

1. WHAT IS YOUR COMPANY'S TRACK RECORD AND REPUTATION IN THE MARKETPLACE?

Reputation matters, but don't take their word for it; ask for references of other landlords with whom they've worked. Ask for at least five names. You may not call them all, but if they have trouble giving you five references, they may not be as good as they sound.

Success in property management translates into leasing homes quickly, choosing good tenants, getting market rent and overseeing daily management at the property. These are the key performance indicators by which you should measure their track record and success.

2. HOW MANY PROPERTIES DOES YOUR COMPANY CURRENTLY MANAGE?

If a company manages fewer than 100 homes, then they don't have the financial resources available to pay for quality advertising that quickly attracts tenants to a property. Under-staffed firms are unable to provide the level of service you need to turn a profit on your rental. Make sure your management firm has access to the systems, people, and revenue required to invest in your rental, just as you have.

3. HOW WILL YOU MARKET MY PROPERTY?

How much money does this management firm spend on advertising the homes it lists versus the other firms you are interviewing? In what media (newspaper, magazine, internet, etc.) does this agent advertise? What do they know about the effectiveness of one medium over the other?

If they can't show you a definite plan and system proven by past results, they are shooting from the hip. Not having systems will produce inconsistent results. You lose money every day your property is vacant on the market, so the marketing plan must be refined, proven, and consistent.

4. WHAT PROPERTIES DOES YOUR COMPANY CURRENTLY LEASE AND MANAGE IN MY AREA?

Managers should be fully aware of their own and other comparable rentals in your area. Again, be attentive to their level of clarity and speed of access to this information. Clarity creates decisiveness, which is absolutely vital to solve the problems that will arise in the management of your rental.

5. DOES YOUR FIRM EXCLUSIVELY MANAGE RESIDENTIAL RENTALS 100% OF THE TIME, OR DO THEY HANDLE PROPERTY MANAGEMENT PART-TIME WHILE SELLING REAL ESTATE?

You will be surprised by how many firms try to get away with this. Why would you want to work with a company that isn't focusing 100% of its time and attention toward residential property management? Some firms actually sell real estate in addition to managing properties. Firms that sell houses in addition to renting and managing are more prone to focus their time and attention on their sales portfolio and

Firms that sell houses in addition to renting and managing are more prone to focus their time and attention on their sales portfolio and large commission.

large commissions rather than their rental portfolio. Success with your rental will come down to you and your team's level of focus, and when it comes to managing your property, it's all or nothing.

6. WHEN YOUR PROPERTIES RENT, ON AVERAGE HOW CLOSE IS THE RENTING PRICE TO THE ASKING PRICE?

Just like you, your property management firm must know its numbers.

"I LOVE HOW YOU: MANAGE 200 PROPERTIES SIMULTANEOUSLY AS THE ONLY EMPLOYEE IN YOUR COMPANY. INSIST ON COLLECTING RENT IN CASH. DON'T BELIEVE IN CONTRACTS OR LEASES EITHER—WE'RE FRIENDS HERE. THINK THAT BEING GRACIOUS TO THE TENANTS WILL MAKE THEM BE GRACIOUS TO US. EVEN THOUGH YOU DON'T HAVE ANY REFERENCES, I'M GOING TO GO WITH MY GUT ON THIS ONE AND HIRE YOU."

Their measurement on this key performance indicator will help you predict how high a price you will get for the rent on your home.

7. ON AVERAGE, HOW LONG DOES IT TAKE FOR YOUR LISTINGS TO RENT?

Does the management firm tend to lease faster or slower than the local average? Do they even track their days on market or is it just a guess? Their performance on this measurement will help you predict how long your home will be on the market before it rents.

8. WHAT HAPPENS IF I'M NOT HAPPY WITH THE JOB YOU ARE DOING TO RENT MY HOME? CAN I CANCEL MY AGREEMENT?

Many management agreements run on a year-by-year basis. Often, management companies will allow for the early cancelation of the agreement. However, they usually have an early termination fee if the client terminates the contract before the end of the agreement. This is similar to cancelling a cell phone contract. The company has invested in staff, equipment, and systems to serve their customer for a period of time. When the customer leaves before the end of the agreement, the company still must honor their agreements with suppliers, employees, etc. Therefore, an early termination fee is charged to help the company cover those overhead costs.

9. WHAT DO YOU DO TO PROMOTE TENANT SATISFACTION?

Tenant satisfaction is key to keeping long-term tenants and slowing turnover. Turnover costs a lot of money, so keeping good tenants for several years is a great way to boost your return on investment. How quickly does the company handle maintenance requests, and how do they handle these requests on weekends or holidays? Do they have a customer appreciation program for tenants?

10. WHAT ARE YOUR FEES?

Often, rental property owners ask this question first. I put this question at the end of the list because that is where it should be. You should also refrain from asking about price up front. Price alone tells you nothing. Price only has meaning when connected to value. You need to first understand what services, quality, and standards the property manager is offering, before you can determine if it is worth paying his or her price. Be wary of the property manager who is the least expensive. Property management is a detailed, frustrating, time consuming job. The manager who is not asking enough for his or her services, has a good chance of going bankrupt, or skipping the details because they simply cannot afford it. Low priced managers simply do not have the money to invest in the systems, technology, and talent needed to provide you with a quality experience and your desired return on investment.

No good parent would hire a daycare without doing considerable due diligence. Interviews, references and history research are a few of the things a good parent does to make sure they are leaving their children in good hands. Think of your property manager as the babysitter or steward of your rental property. Once your property has been purchased, your main job is to protect your investment. The right property manager will help you do this but the wrong one could very well derail your entire vision.

Take your time. Do your due diligence. Then make your move.

CHAPTER 8
Rent Your Home Quickly

You may have been expecting this chapter to be a lot longer than it is. The truth about getting your home rented quickly to the right tenants is very simple; however, the execution is not. As in anything else with your rental, strategic and systematic consistency is the only way you will win. Take the simple ideas in this chapter and systemize them because renting your home quickly for the maximum amount should be your and your property manager's absolute top priority.

To rent your home quickly and turn a profit, you must consider and balance the following three interconnected components during the advertising and showing process.

PRICE

Although we view every home we manage as unique, unfortunately the rental market sees your home as a commodity, and supply and demand dictates the price you receive for your home. Prices fluctuate with economic conditions, seasons of the year, the number of competing properties on the market, and the number of qualified tenants looking to rent.

TIME

Your own personal timeline will dictate the amount of flexibility you have as it relates to the price you receive for your home. The more quickly you need a tenant, the more aggressively you will need to price the property.

TENANT QUALIFICATIONS

You need quality tenants to occupy your property for many reasons. Having stringent qualifications might deter some possible tenants from applying but will save you in the long run from late rent payments, property damage, evictions, etc.

> **Having stringent qualifications might deter some possible tenants from applying but will save you in the long run.**

You must become an expert at balancing price, timeline, and tenant qualifications to maximize your rental rate and minimize your vacancy time. The key to this is numbers and context. Know your numbers, analyze the circumstances, and rent your property quickly. Here are three potential scenarios you could face and what could happen as a result.

Rental Rate is Set Too High:

- *Showings on the property will be slow. Potential tenants will realize it's overpriced and will not even call to schedule a showing let alone make an application on the home. The home will sit vacant for a longer period of time costing you more and more money each day.*

You Need it Rented Fast:

- *This means you will have to be aggressive on price relative to the other competing homes. The rental rate will have to scream "value."*

Tenant Qualifications are Too Low:

- *The home may rent quickly and even at the upper end of the price range. However, the tenants placed are most likely "high risk" tenants with an increased risk of missed rent payments, evictions, legal problems, etc.*

Systems are the only things that create consistency when it comes to managing your property. What are your systems for getting your property rented the fastest with the highest quality tenant possible? Are your systems based on theory or proven past results? Put in the time, make the systems and put them into action.

CHAPTER 9
Consistently Receiving Rent Payments

You've heard it before: Cash is king. Cash flow is the air supply of a business. Zig Ziglar once said that money is like oxygen because when you need it, you really need it. In order to keep your business running optimally, you must have consistent rent collections. Assuring the cash flow moving consistently is an area of your business you will never take your eyes off but that doesn't mean you need to lose sleep over it. Implement these strategies for your rent payments and you will keep the oxygen levels at 100% for your rental investment.

RELIABLE TENANTS

Find quality tenants with good credit and enough income to afford the rent. Credit has to do with the quality of the person, while income has to do with the ability of the person. For example, even though a person has an excellent credit score, they may not make enough money to afford the rent or may have too many other expenses to cover, thus reducing their ability to pay. My standard rent to income ratio is 30% for cheaper properties and up to 40% on more expensive properties. Set your standards, and stick to them. When your property is on the market and you are thinking about dipping into savings to make the mortgage payment, it will be emotionally tempting to bend the rules and lower the bar, but don't give in. You can change your standards from time to time. But when you do, try not to do it in the heat of the moment. Implement a thoughtful, systematic change.

CLEAR EXPECTATIONS

Clear expectations from the beginning will save a major headache in the end (or even litigation). Have a clear conversation with your new tenant about what the lease agreement means. Don't cut corners or shorten the conversation just because of the excitement you both have about signing the agreement. Slow down and express that you are happy to be working with them, but also let them know this is a serious agreement with serious consequences. Make sure they understand the consequences, without dampening their excitement for their new home.

NO GRACE IN PROPERTY MANAGEMENT

Communicate the consequences of late rental payments, and follow through with them every time. Your tenants will test your boundaries, and when it comes to money, if you give them an inch, they will take it. Remember, money is an emotional subject for your tenant and for you. It's natural to feel like the bad guy or to be passive, but if you set very clear expectations, you will be surprised as to how this improves your relationship with your tenant. It's like creating a personal budget. While at first you may think that implementing a budget is rigid and limiting, you will likely find as others have that a budget actually creates a sense of clarity and freedom. This applies directly to ensuring your tenants understand your boundaries. A quality landlord clearly communicates the rules, and a quality tenant appreciates them.

> *Your tenants will test your boundaries, and when it comes to money, if you give them an inch, they will take it.*

BE DISCIPLINED WITH THE COLLECTIONS TIME LINE

Once the statutory grace period is over, immediately start the eviction process. This doesn't mean you have to evict, but initiate the process in case they don't pay. This communicates to your tenant that you are serious, and this is the process you are required to follow.

AUTOMATIC PAYMENTS

Consider requiring direct withdrawal of rent from your tenant's checking account. This empowers your tenant to appropriately prioritize their rent payment. Since shelter is key to basic survival, it is a top priority and should be the first bill that is paid. They should pay their rent before they pay their phone, food, electric or TV bill. By offering the direct withdrawal, you can avoid some uncomfortable situations.

NON-SUFFICIENT FUNDS

Once a tenant has passed off a NSF (non-sufficient funds) check, require certified funds such as a money order or cashier's check as the only method of payment from that day forward. If they did it once, they will probably try to do it again. This will free your mind from extra and unnecessary worry each month until the check clears.

NEVER ACCEPT CASH

If you accept a cash payment, then you will have to meet your tenant personally in order for them to pay. This directly cuts into your profits because of the additional time and expense required to meet them and also poses issues related to safety and accounting. Being handed a wad of cash could eventually threaten your safety; how long before someone mugs you to get your cash? Accounting will remain an issue as well because cash is hard to account for, and the probability of miscounting cash increases as the amount of cash handled increases. Cash payments also leave you vulnerable in terms of proof of payment. If a tenant pays in cash, how do you prove they did or did not pay?

CREDIT CARD PAYMENTS

Allowing your tenants to pay their rent online by offering credit card payments is a good collection solution. This makes it easy for your tenant, but make sure to add a convenience fee to cover the transaction fee the credit card company will charge you.

When it comes to collecting rent, there are a lot of things to think about, but not a lot of things to worry about as long as you put the right systems in place. The less you have to worry about cash flow the more you can build your investment portfolio.

Do's and don'ts for qualifying good tenants

Don't stereotype. Qualified and unqualified tenants come from every age, race, gender, and background.

Do check their credit.

Do run state and national criminal checks.

Do run a sex offender check.

Do ask for the applicant's last two pay stubs.

Do call the previous landlords and ask them about their experience with your potential tenants.

Do have a set of standards for accepting and declining applicants. This will help eliminate your emotions.

Standards by which you should abide:

- *Rent to income ratio 30-40%*
- *Will you accept felons? If so, which ones and timeline from last offense?*
- *Will you accept people with drug crimes on their records? If so, which ones and timeline from last offense?*
- *What is your criteria for acceptance on the applicant's credit report?*
- *Will you accept sex offenders? If so, pay attention to the laws about a sex offender's proximity to a school.*
- *Will you require someone over 21 be on the lease?*

Even after you read a book or take a class on tenant qualification, you might still fail at this task. Tenant qualification is an art and a skill that requires a combination of knowledge and experience to master. I think of tenant qualification as a stew. You will need to know some laws, have some people skills, have the ability to pick up on small details (like how they take care of their car), have an ear for key words, have some technical underwriting skills, do some detective work, and read body languages for certain behaviors. Then mix all the ingredients into the stew and keep adding salt and pepper ingredients because some tenants are "professionals" at getting passed even the most trained and experienced leasing agents.

7 Tips to Avoid Tenant Trouble

1 See the opportunity within the problem. Resolutions begin with your attitude and approach to the situation. Relationships are strengthened during disputes and troubles if they are handled appropriately. If you handle this dispute correctly and professionally, your relationship with your tenant can actually become stronger. The better relationship you have with your tenant, the more likely they are going to remain your tenant in the future.

2 Follow the Golden Rule. Treat your tenant the way you want to be treated. Your tenant is your customer. Without your tenant, you have no income and no profit.

3. At the beginning of the conversation, inform your tenant that you are committed to finding a solution. Remind them you both are on the same team. This doesn't mean you will give them everything they want, but it will get their guard down and communication open.

4. Seek to understand before seeking to be understood. Their complaint may not be serious, but they believe it is serious. Through listening, you are empathizing and valuing their opinion. Ask straightforward and open-ended questions so you can understand exactly what the real problem is.

5. Don't rely on your memory; rely on your objective documentation. Anytime there is a dispute or complaint, document it. If the matter ends up in court, your documentation is admissible as evidence.

6. Once you understand the entire complaint or dispute, ask your tenant what they think is the best solution. Often your tenant knows how they want to handle the dispute. When you ask for their solutions first, you are again showing them you value their opinion, and many times their solution is more advantageous for you.

7. Once you have listened to your tenant's proposed solution, you can begin negotiating from this point forward.

Next Steps

Now that you've read the good and bad along with the ups and downs, I want to leave you with one final thought: Remember.

Remember why you wanted to invest in rental properties in the first place. I'm not just talking about the money (though that certainly is a big deal), but remember what the money will get you – that's why you started. Our motivations in life are not as much about the thing we are after as it is the feeling we get from the people we provide for and go through life with. Remember why you started in the first place because your resolve will be tested time and time again.

Remember for whom you are doing all this work, for whom you are investing and putting in the long hours. The ultimate measure of success will always come back to people, not so much the volume of our bank account, but the quality of our relationships. Don't get me wrong. I love seeing good numbers in my bank account, but I can assure you that I love my wife much more. I love my children being healthy and knowing their dad is always there for them.

Do whatever you need to do to remember the people for whom you are doing this work - your spouse, your children, your grandchildren, your great-grandchildren. Whether they are here right now or not, remember these people because I guarantee you that all the accomplishments in the world will not matter if your relationships don't flourish with your financial success.

It's really simple. Get the right plan, get the right team, and get to work. *You can do this, there is no doubt!* Just never quit trying.

Suggested Reading

I mentioned several times that training and education is one of the keys to success. I always appreciate book recommendations from others, so here are a few titles that have helped grow my knowledge in business, real estate, and investing.

Start with Why by Simon Sinek

The E-Myth Revisited by Michael E Gerber

Good to Great by Jim Collins

Great by Choice by Jim Collins

Rich Dad Poor Dad Robert T. Kiyosaki

How to Win Friends and Influence People by Dale Carnegie

Atlas Shrugged by Ayn Rand

Entreleadership by Dave Ramsey

The Entrepreneur Equation by Carol Roth

About the Authors

Josh Kattenberg
josh@expressrpm.com
605.274.7373
www.ExpressRPM.com
Twitter: @RPMSiouxFalls
Facebook.com/ExpressRPM

Josh is the owner/CEO of Real Property Management Express which provides full service residential property management services to the Sioux Falls, SD community and is responsible for a real estate portfolio worth more than $20,000,000. The Real Property Management family made the Inc. Magazine 500 list of the fastest growing companies in America for the past 4 years and Real Property Management Express has received the Franchisee of the Year Award and has been voted The Local Best for the Sioux Falls area. As an entrepreneur, Josh started a construction company building custom homes right out of high school, and was instrumental in opening and operating a private high school. Josh continues to teach in a number of ways including presenting continuing education classes for property managers, leading Dave Ramsey money management courses for the community, and is a regular contributor to his own blog as well as blogs for entrepreneurs and business leaders. Josh has been and continues to be involved in his community with various organizations such as a volunteer for The American Red Cross, as an EMT for Hull Ambulance, as the chairman and teacher for an inner city mission and more. For his undergrad, he majored in Ancient Studies which included ancient history, archeology, and oodles of languages—Latin, Greek, Hebrew, Egyptian Hieroglyphics, Coptic, and French. He has a master's degree in Education. In his spare time Josh enjoys rock climbing The Needles in the Black Hills, playing Ultimate Frisbee and Racquetball, and flying. Josh and his wife Sharla have two elementary aged children, Willem and Sarsih.

Derek is the co-owner of Real Property Management Express. He is known for his contagious laugh and warm smile. He is able to make friends and build loyalty wherever he goes. For ten years he was an ASE Master Certified Auto Technician and Shop Manager. He has an ability to see through problems and find the best solution. As a technician he often would go against the suggested "manual" process and save his clients time and money.

Derek believes in volunteering in his community and enjoys helping other business owners grow their business. He is on the Ambassador Committee for the Sioux Falls Chamber. As an ambassador he teaches business owners the value of being part of the local chamber and helps them connect with other business owners. He volunteers for the South Dakota Multi Housing Association helping educate property owners and create a property owner friendly environment. He also helps with the Scholarship committee for the Sales and Marketing Executives which gives scholarships to college students going to school for business and marketing.

Derek Kattenberg
derek@expressrpm.com
605.274.7373
www.ExpressRPM.com
Twitter: @RPMSiouxFalls
Facebook.com/ExpressRPM

Derek's ability to connect and build relationships has helped Real Property Management Express grow quickly through referrals. After hours Derek enjoys many outdoor activities including golfing, snowmobiling and working on projects in his shop. He lives on an acreage by Brandon, SD with Laura, his wife of 9 years and their Chocolate lab Rogan.

Testimonials

"Real Property Management Express has been an excellent resource for me, as a Real Estate Professional when working with clients to lease their property or to help home renters with a property that I know will be professionally managed by Derek and Josh."

Liz Lloyd
Broker, Vice President of Real Estate
Lloyd Residential Group

"The first time I met Josh and Derek, it was easy to tell they have a passion for what they do. They put their property owners and tenants first and are committed to their success."

Keith Severson
Partner, Eide Bailey
Chair of the Board, Sioux Falls Chamber of Commerce

"I send every referral I can to Derek and Josh. They have an understanding of what it takes to make an investment property work, and they provide great customer service!"

Tyler Goff
Buyer and Seller Expert, Hegg REALTORS®, Inc.

"I can always count on Josh and Derek to follow through with their word and in today's world, that is a rare and valuable trait."

Vince Jones
Shareholder, Woods, Fuller, Shultz & Smith P.C.